MONTVILLE TWP. PUBLIC LIBRARY
90 Horseneck Road
Montville, N.J. 07045

W9-ASE-797

0 1021 0170772 1

ON LINE

JBIOG
Paste
Spengler, Kenneth

Louis Pasteur

Montville Township Public Library
90 Horseneck Road
Montville, N.J. 07045-9626

<u>Library Hours</u>
Monday	10 a.m. - 9 p.m.
Tuesday	10 a.m. - 9 p.m.
Wednesday	1 p.m. - 9 p.m.
Thursday	10 a.m. - 9 p.m.
Friday	10 a.m. - 5 p.m.
Saturday	10 a.m. - 5 p.m.
Sunday	1 p.m. - 5 p.m.

Closed Sundays
Memorial Day through Labor Day

Louis Pasteur

A Photo-Illustrated Biography

by Kremena Spengler

Consultant:
David V. Cohn, Ph.D.
Biomedical Research Consultant and
Emeritus Professor of Biochemistry
University of Louisville

Bridgestone Books
an imprint of Capstone Press
Mankato, Minnesota

Bridgestone Books are published by Capstone Press
151 Good Counsel Drive, P.O. Box 669, Mankato, Minnesota 56002
http://www.capstone-press.com

Copyright © 2004 Capstone Press. All rights reserved.
No part of this publication may be reproduced in whole or in part, or stored in a retrieval
system, or transmitted in any form or by any means, electronic, mechanical, photocopying,
recording, or otherwise, without written permission of the publisher.
For infomation regarding permission, write to Capstone Press,
151 Good Counsel Drive, P. O. Box 669, Dept R, Mankato, Minnesota 56002.
Printed in the United States of America

Library of Congress Cataloging-in-Publication Data
Spengler, Kremena.
    Louis Pasteur / by Kremena Spengler.
    v. cm.—(A photo-illustrated biography)
    Contents: Fighter of disease—Childhood and education—Early work and marriage
Studying beet juice—Growing germs—Helping the silk industry—Fighting diseases— A
vaccine for rabies—Later years—Fast facts about Louis Pasteur—Dates in Louis Pasteur's
life.
    ISBN 0-7368-2225-9
    1. Pasteur, Louis, 1822–1895—Juvenile literature. 2. Scientists—France—Biography—
juvenile literature. 3. Microbiologists—France—Biography—Juvenile literature. [1. Pasteur,
Louis, 1822–1895. 2. Scientists. 3. Microbiologists.] I. Title. II. Series: Photo-illustrated
biographies.
    Q143.P2S63 2004
    579'.092—dc21   2003002549

Editorial credits
Wendy M. Dieker, editor; Enoch Peterson, cover designer and interior illustrator; Steve
    Christensen, series designer; Kelly Garvin, photo researcher; Karen Risch, product
    planning editor

Photo credits
Corbis/Hulton-Deutsch Collection, cover
Getty Images/Hulton Archive, 12, 14, 20
Institute Pasteur, 6, 8
Stock Montage, Inc., 4, 10, 16, 18

1 2 3 4 5 6 08 07 06 05 04 03

0 1021 0170772 1

Table of Contents

"Chance favors only the prepared mind."
–Louis, in a speech at the University of Lille, 1854

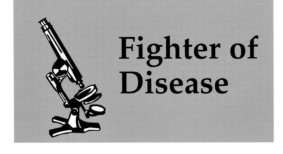

Fighter of Disease

In the late 1800s, French scientist Louis Pasteur (pass-TUR) studied tiny living beings called germs. Louis discovered that germs can cause diseases.

Louis found a new way to fight diseases. He gave people shots of weakened or dead germs. These shots, called vaccines, helped people's bodies fight off diseases.

Another important discovery Louis made was a way to keep milk and other foods from spoiling too quickly. This process is called pasteurization. Pasteurized foods can be kept for several days before spoiling.

Animals also have better lives because of Louis' work. He studied and prevented diseases in silkworms, sheep, and chickens. Louis also found a vaccine for rabies, a deadly disease spread to both animals and humans.

Louis Pasteur invented ways to keep food fresh and to help people fight diseases.

Childhood and Education

Louis was born December 27, 1822, in France. His father, Jean-Joseph, worked with leather. His mother, Jeanne-Etiennette, cared for the home and family. Louis had three sisters.

As a young boy, Louis was an average student. His main talent was art. He drew pictures of his parents and friends.

Louis started to like science in high school. His father urged him to be a teacher. Louis graduated from college in 1842. But he still needed more schooling to be a teacher.

In 1843, Louis entered the École Normale Supérieure in Paris. It was the best school for science teachers in France.

Louis passed the teaching tests in 1846. But he decided to stay at the École Normale to study. Louis completed his science studies in 1847.

Louis' friend drew this picture of him at the École Normale. They studied science together at school.

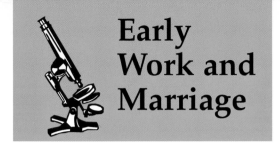

Early Work and Marriage

After finishing school, Louis became a professor's assistant. He studied crystals. Crystals often form when water and other liquids harden. Louis learned why some crystals bend light and others do not.

Louis' work with crystals earned him a job as a chemistry professor. He taught for a short time in Dijon, France. He started teaching chemistry at Strasbourg University in France in 1849.

In Strasbourg, Louis fell in love with Marie Laurent. Her father was the head of the university. Louis and Marie were married May 29, 1849.

Marie often helped Louis keep working. She was Louis' secretary. She also supported him when he would get discouraged.

The Pasteurs had five children. Three of Louis' daughters died in childhood from diseases. People think their deaths made Louis want to study germs.

Louis and Marie were married for 46 years.

" . . . to wonder and question is the first step of the mind toward discovery."
–Louis, in a lecture about science, 1883

Studying Beet Juice

In 1854, Louis became a professor at the University of Lille in northern France. His research there helped local companies.

Workers in Lille made alcohol from beet juice. The alcohol sometimes spoiled. The workers asked Louis to study the process that turns beet juice into alcohol. Louis showed that germs cause the alcohol from beet juice to spoil.

This research earned Louis respect and fame. In 1857, he became director of scientific studies at his old school, the École Normale.

Louis continued to study germs in food. He found that germs turn milk sour and make wine taste bad. By 1864, Louis learned to heat food for a few minutes to kill the germs. This process was named "pasteurization" after Louis. People still use pasteurization today to keep food fresh.

Louis looked at alcohol under a microscope. He found germs that made the alcohol spoil.

11

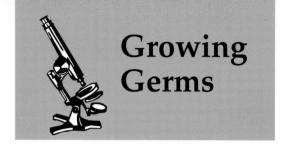

Growing Germs

Louis was not the only person interested in germs. In the 1860s, many scientists studied germs. They argued about where germs came from. Some scientists believed that germs grew from dead matter. Louis did not agree with those scientists. He believed that germs were in the air. He thought that these germs created new germs.

In 1864, Louis tried to prove his theory. He put some liquid in a glass bottle. Then, he bent the neck of the bottle down and up again into an S shape. Louis boiled the liquid to kill the germs. When air came into the bottle, the germs were trapped in the bent neck. After a while, there were still no germs in the liquid. Then, Louis tipped the bottle to let the liquid touch the germs in the neck. Germs soon grew in the liquid. This experiment proved that germs came from other germs in the air.

Louis used a machine called a sterilizer to boil the liquids he studied and kill the germs.

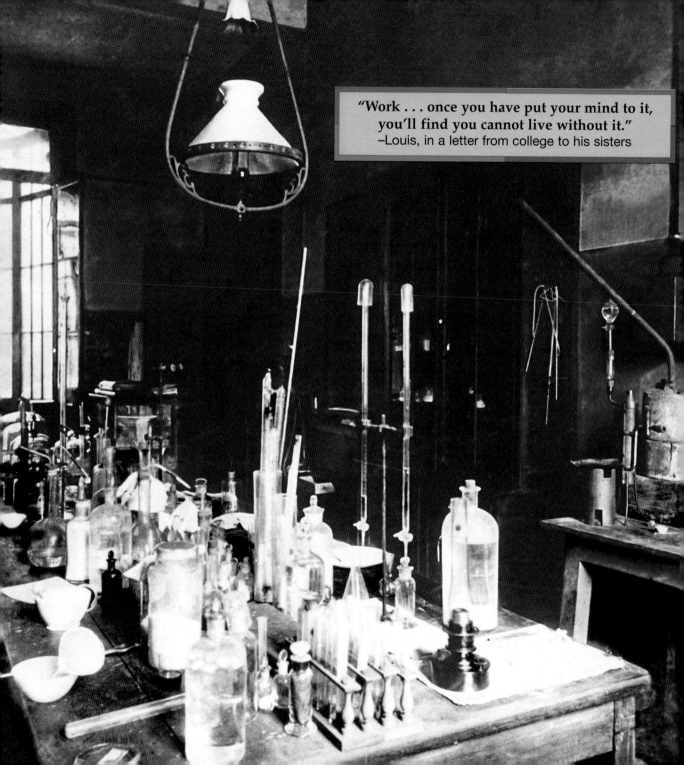

"Work . . . once you have put your mind to it, you'll find you cannot live without it."
–Louis, in a letter from college to his sisters

Helping the Silk Industry

In the 1860s, a disease killed many silkworms in Europe. In 1865, Louis traveled to Alès in southern France to help the silk farmers. Louis spent five summers in Alès.

Louis found two germs that attacked the silkworms and made them sick. Louis taught farmers to destroy the sick worms and only breed the healthy ones. Louis' research helped save the French silk industry.

Each fall, Louis returned to the École Normale to teach classes. In 1867, Louis became director of the school's new chemistry laboratory. He also started teaching classes at the Sorbonne University in Paris, France.

In 1868, Louis suffered a stroke. The stroke made him unable to move the left side of his body. He never healed completely, but he kept working.

Many bottles and jars filled Louis' laboratory at the École Normale.

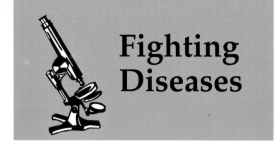

Fighting Diseases

In 1877, Louis argued that germs caused and spread deadly diseases. This idea became known as "the germ theory of disease."

One disease that Louis studied was chicken cholera. In his lab, he grew the germs that caused the disease. He gave some chickens shots of the germs, and they soon died.

One time, the germs weakened before he could give them to the chickens. Louis injected these weak germs into some chickens. The weak germs did not kill the chickens. When these chickens later received shots of new, strong germs, they stayed healthy.

Louis figured out that shots of weakened and dead germs could help animals fight disease. The weakened or dead germs are called vaccines. In 1880, Louis made a chicken cholera vaccine. Later, he made a vaccine for a sheep disease called anthrax.

Louis spent hours in his laboratory studying germs.

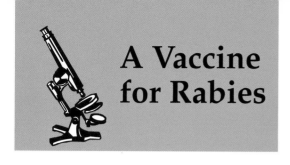

A Vaccine for Rabies

Louis decided to find vaccines to help people. He studied a deadly disease called rabies. People can catch rabies from the bite of a rabid animal.

Louis made a vaccine and tested it on dogs and other animals. The vaccine was working on the animals in his laboratory. He did not think it was time to try it on people. But in 1885, a boy named Joseph Meister came to his office. A dog with rabies had bitten the boy. Louis agreed to vaccinate him.

Joseph received several shots of the vaccine. Louis wanted to help the boy's body slowly fight the rabies germs. The vaccine worked, and Joseph lived.

A few months later, Louis helped vaccinate 15-year-old Jean-Baptiste Jupille. Jean-Baptiste fought a rabid dog to save some younger children. The dog bit Jean-Baptiste several times. Louis' vaccine also saved him.

Louis watched as Jean-Baptiste Jupille (seated) received several shots of the rabies vaccine.

Later Years

Louis continued to work hard, but his health failed. In 1887, he suffered another stroke. Louis could hardly walk by himself.

The French government honored Louis in 1888. They built a center in Paris to study germ-spread diseases. The government named it the Pastuer Institute. Louis was the head of the institute for almost seven years.

Louis died on September 28, 1895. Thousands of people attended his funeral. Louis is now buried in a beautifully decorated tomb at the Pasteur Institute.

Louis' work helped improve people's lives. Pasteurization is still used to make foods safe. The germ theory greatly changed how doctors treat diseases. Vaccines spare millions of people from sicknesses and death. Louis' discoveries continue to help people around the world.

Joseph Lister (foreground) greeted Louis (second from left) at a gathering to honor Louis' work.

Fast Facts about Louis Pasteur

 In 1838, Louis left for school in Paris. But he was very homesick. His father brought him home within a month.

 Louis won more than 20 honors, prizes, and awards for his research and discoveries in science.

 The Pasteur Institute continues to study germs. It was one of the first research centers to find the germ that causes AIDS.

Dates in Louis Pasteur's Life

1822—Louis is born December 27 in Dole, France.

1843—Louis begins studies at the École Normale Supérieure in Paris.

1849—Louis marries Marie Laurent May 29 in Strasbourg.

1854—Louis is a director at the University of Lille; he studies beet juice.

1864—Louis argues that germs come from other germs; he invents pasteurization.

1865—Louis begins studies of silkworm diseases in Alès.

1868—Louis has his first stroke.

1880—Louis invents a chicken cholera vaccine.

1885—Louis helps vaccinate two boys against rabies.

1887—Louis has his second stroke.

1888—Louis heads the newly opened Pasteur Institute in Paris.

1895—Louis dies September 28 in Paris.

Words to Know

alcohol (AL-kuh-hol)—a substance formed when sugar breaks down
anthrax (AN-thraks)—a sheep disease that can spread to people
chicken cholera (CHIK-uhn KOL-ur-uh)—a deadly disease in chickens
crystal (KRISS-tuhl)—a hard substance that forms when water or other liquids harden; salt and snowflakes are crystals.
germ (JURM)—a tiny living being that causes diseases or food spoilage
pasteurize (PASS-chuh-rize)—the process of heating milk or other foods long enough to kill the germs
rabies (RAY-beez)—a deadly disease that people and animals can get from the bite of an infected animal; an animal with rabies is rabid.
vaccine (vak-SEEN)—dead or weakened germs injected into a person or animal to help fight diseases

Read More

Armentrout, David, and Patricia Armentrout. *Louis Pasteur.* People Who Made a Difference. Vero Beach, Fla.: Rourke, 2002.

Fullick, Ann. *Louis Pasteur.* Groundbreakers. Chicago: Heinemann Library, 2001.

Nardo, Don. *Germs.* The Kidhaven Science Library. San Diego: Kidhaven Press, 2002.

Useful Addresses

American Society for Microbiology
1752 N Street NW
Washington, D.C. 20036

Pasteur Institute
25-28 rue Du Dr Roux
75015 Paris, France

Internet Sites

Do you want to find out more about Louis Pasteur?
Let FactHound, our fact-finding hound dog, do the research for you!

Here's how:

1) Visit *http://www.facthound.com*
2) Type in the **BOOK ID** number: **0736822259**
3) Click on **FETCH IT**.

FactHound will fetch Internet sites picked by our editors just for you!

Index

MONTVILLE TWP. PUBLIC LIBRARY
90 Horseneck Road
Montville, N.J. 07045